W0038401

Divide and Conquer or Divide and Subdivide?
How Not to Refight the First International

Mark Leier

PM Press Pamphlet Series No. 0015
Divide and Conquer or Divide and Subdivide? How Not to Refight the First International
Mark Leier

ISBN: 978-1-62963-383-1

Copyright © 2017
This edition copyright PM Press
All rights reserved

PM Press
PO Box 23912
Oakland, CA 94623
www.pmpress.org

Printed in Oakland, CA, on recycled paper with soy ink.

DIVIDE AND CONQUER OR DIVIDE AND SUBDIVIDE?
HOW NOT TO REFIGHT THE FIRST INTERNATIONAL
MARK LEIER

SINCE THE FIGHTS BETWEEN BAKUNIN AND MARX IN THE FIRST International in 1864, anarchists and Marxists have emphasized the differences between the two. Even their physical stature was different. Bakunin was large, standing six feet four inches tall and weighing perhaps three hundred pounds, with a fair complexion and blond hair. Marx was short and dark, reflecting his family nickname of "The Moor." Other characteristics, however, emphasize how much they resembled each other. In the few, posed black-and-white photographs that have been preserved, which, appropriately enough, look rather like mug shots, it is difficult for the casual observer to distinguish one from the other. Both adopt the formal, stiff posture fashionable for photographs of the time, and each has a portly build, unkempt hair, and an unruly beard. Both are dressed in the formal, sloppy manner befitting slightly disreputable members of the Victorian intelligentsia, and they even patronized the same London tailor for a time.

For two men who fought so bitterly, their similarities go much deeper than physical appearance, grooming, and clothing. They were close in age—Bakunin born in 1814, Marx four years later—and so grew up in a shared intellectual, political, and cultural climate. More importantly, their family backgrounds gave them similar opportunities and experiences. Bakunin's family was part of the Russian nobility, but that description may hide more than it reveals. Russia was essentially a feudal society, and the wealth of the Bakunin family came from the peasantry, the serfs who were bound to lord and land. But the

1

family was not of the grand aristocracy. The Bakunin estate was at Priamukhino, far from the political and cultural centers of Moscow and St. Petersburg and far from the swirl and opportunities of the tsar's court. The Bakunins were not wealthy but had obtained admission to the ranks of the aristocracy through service to the tsar, in much the way Lenin's family would years later. This is not to underestimate the relative privilege of the Bakunin family or the power it held over the serfs that worked the land. It did mean, however, that Bakunin and his sisters and brothers were not part of the idle rich. There was money for education, but education was instrumental, aimed at equipping the daughters to marry well and to train the sons for service in the officer corps or government office. While the children were afforded an excellent education and cultural accoutrements of their class such as music and language lessons, money was always a concern. Pennies had to be watched, debt avoided, and sacrifices made.

Marx's family too was somewhere in the middle ranks of German society. His father owned vineyards, but it was his work as an attorney that provided the family income, and like Bakunin's family, maintaining their social position meant watching expenses carefully and investing in education to give the children what is sometimes called "social capital." Again like the Bakunin family, the Marxes were not part of the inner circles of power of German society. Born in Catholic Trier shortly after the city was ceded from France to Prussia, Karl Marx was baptized a Lutheran, but his father had recently converted from Judaism. This separated the family from the conservative, traditional elites of Prussia as effectively as the isolation of Priamukhino separated the Bakunins from the elites of Russia.

Thus both men undeniably came from privileged backgrounds, but the privilege was narrowly bound, dependent not on great wealth but on relatively modest means and the access to education those means and status made possible. As the oldest male children, Michael Bakunin and Karl Marx had great expectations put on them. In Bakunin's case, a career as a military officer would open up doors in government service and give him the managerial skills to run the estate. For Marx, the hope was that he would study law. Both received excellent early educations at home, learning several languages, mathematics, and literature. They learned other lessons at home as well. Neither of their fathers were radicals or revolutionaries, but both men were products of the Enlightenment and loosely connected to progressive causes. Alexander Bakunin had associated with people with ties to the Decembrist movement, a group of army officers who agitated for a constitutional monarchy and the abolition of serfdom in 1825. Heinrich Marx too was part of a circle of reformers pushing for modest constitutional reform. Their political ideals may be characterized as cautious liberalization of their respective political regimes, changes that would give people, especially those of their classes, more breathing room, freer exchanges of ideas, and more access to power without upsetting society or causing turmoil. And both men retreated rather hastily when the conservative state pushed back. Nonetheless, they gave their children much more than an uncritical, patriotic, conservative upbringing.

Both fathers came to regret it. In 1828, Michael Bakunin was sent off to school in St. Petersburg, first to a sort of prep school then to military academy to train to become an artillery officer. He was an unhappy and sometimes unruly cadet, whose studies were marked with a great deal of indolence and frantic cramming at exam time. Despite his undistinguished performance, he was commissioned as an officer in 1832. In 1830, Marx entered high school. He graduated in 1835 with average grades, notably and ironically weak in history, and went to the University of Bonn to study law. So far, both young men seemed dutiful sons of the middle class, competent but not exemplary students with the potential for solid careers in the state and civil bureaucracies.

That illusion was quickly dispelled. The first sign was their inability to manage money. Both men piled up debts, never for the books or tutoring or school supplies their families would have cheerfully scrimped to provide, but for lavish meals, alcohol, parties, concerts, and plays. Letters begging for more money were met with parental warnings to be responsible, accountable, and above all, studious. As is usually the case in such matters, the warnings were ignored.

It got worse. After three years of service, each of which he loathed, Bakunin left the military. He did not formally resign; he simply went AWOL, leaving his parents to use what little influence they had to secure his formal resignation by falsely claiming he was ill. Marx's rebellion was less fraught but no less alarming; he left Bonn for the University of Berlin, where he hoped to become a poet. He proved no more adept at verse than Bakunin had at military service.

By 1836, each had taken up an even more disreputable pursuit: philosophy. Bakunin moved to Moscow where he became part of a literary and philosophy circle named after Nikolai Stankevich, a young poet, critic, and liberal humanist. There Bakunin was joined by his sisters, Liubov, Varvara, Tatiana, and Alexandra, who were themselves influential members of the Stankevich circle. Other members of the loosely knit critical group included the literary critic Vissarion Belinsky and the political writer Alexander Herzen. Literature, philosophy, and politics intertwined and were debated long through the night. For his part, Marx started in law at Berlin, but became much more interested in the philosophy of law than formal, practical legal studies. Their parents were dismayed as their sons took up such idle pursuits—after all, what does one do with a degree in philosophy? Nor were the parents pleased when both took up the study of the most controversial philosopher of the day: Hegel.

It is difficult today to appreciate the impact Hegel had on the men and women of Bakunin and Marx's generation. Theirs was a Europe in flux, as the old verities of the feudal world were being swept away by industrial capitalism and its new forms of exploitation. Revolutions in thought and politics accompanied the transition in the economies as new groups and classes sought political power from the point of a sword and the barrel of a gun and with new ideologies and new political constitutions. Hegel championed this new world, a world not of stability and order and fixed place but one of chaos and opportunity and mobility. In his view, history, and so the future, were marked by transformation, not stasis. No political regime was fixed or unassailable, no economic system was permanent or immutable, no one's status was inevitable or fixed. History, according to Hegel, or at least some of his interpreters, was on the side of unrest and motion. This was a philosophy that appealed to those who wished to change society—as Herzen put it, Hegel had given them the "algebra of revolution" with his arguments about the evolution of humanity and its progressive search for freedom. Such a philosophy appealed greatly to Bakunin and to Marx and they soon proclaimed themselves Hegelians.

In 1838, Bakunin wrote a preface to a translation of Hegel's *Gymnasium Lectures* and followed this up with a two-part article, "On Philosophy," in 1840. In the essays, Bakunin asserted that history—humanity—was propelled by "the contradiction between the infinity of [humanity's] internal ideal essence and the limitation of his external existence; contradiction is the source of movement, of development, striving only towards its resolution."[1] Humanity's ideal essence was, in his view and Hegel's, the striving for freedom, and for Bakunin, that meant more than freedom of thought—it meant political and economic freedom as well. Philosophy was important, but only to the degree that it combined with action to produce changes in real human lives.

Marx, of course, was moving in the same direction, from abstract, if critical, philosophy to politics. As members of the left-leaning Young Hegelians, a group of university students and professors, he and Friedrich Engels would later denounce abstract analysis, declaring in *The German Ideology* that "philosophy and the study of the actual world have the same relation to one another as onanism and sexual love."[2] For his part, Bakunin observed that "noise, empty chatter—this is the only result of the awful, senseless anarchy of minds

5

which constitutes the main illness of our new generation—a generation that is abstract, illusory, and foreign to any reality."[3] Philosophy could not remain in the lecture hall and seminar room. It had to return to the real world, and that meant politics.

Political thought and action were much more advanced and accessible in Europe than in the tsar's Russia, and so Bakunin went to the University of Berlin in 1840, hoping to complete a doctorate and find work as a university lecturer. He fell in with an impressive group of students that included Engels, Kaspar Schmidt (better known as Max Stirner), and Søren Kierkegaard. Another was the Russian novelist Ivan Turgenev, who would later draw upon Bakunin for the title character of his novel *Rudin*.

Marx too was a student there, finishing his doctoral dissertation "The Difference between the Democritean and Epicurean Philosophy of Nature, with an Appendix." Deep in his studies, he met neither Bakunin nor Engels. Despite Marx's early promise as a philosopher, his plans for a university career were thwarted when one of his mentors, Bruno Bauer, lost his position at the University of Bonn as part of the state's repression of the Left and of Hegelians in high places.

By 1842, it was clear that neither Marx nor Bakunin would find careers in the academy. They turned to journalism and politics instead. Neither was yet a socialist; it would be more accurate to describe them as radical democrats. But their views were shifting. Each was influenced by Lorenz von Stein's book, *The Socialism and Communism of Present-Day France*. Originally an investigation commissioned by the Prussian government, the book was a warning against socialism, not an argument for it, but it soon became popular among left-leaning intellectuals in Germany. Von Stein was a university professor and something of a Hegelian, though a conservative one, and stressed the importance of economic matters in history and politics. Read against the grain—easy work for young dialectical Hegelian rebels—von Stein illustrated how a working-class movement had developed in France and pointed to the possibility of a more democratic and more progressive future led by workers and intellectuals. After all, while Germans argued and wrote and debated idealist philosophy, France had looked to political economy and material interests to make a successful revolution in 1789 and to launch a series of rebellions and uprisings in the 1830s, notably the June Rebellion immortalized by Victor Hugo in his novel *Les Misérables.*

Turning from philosophy to popular politics, Bakunin and Marx wrote for a new journal, the *Deutsche Jahrbücher*, edited by Arnold Ruge. Ruge was several years older than Bakunin and Marx and had been imprisoned during his student days for his political action. He was a Hegelian and that too made him a marked man. When he was denied a chair at the University of Halle, he abandoned academia and founded a series of left-leaning journals. The journals took up questions of constitutional democracy, state policy, political reform, socialism, literature, and art, usually from a liberal, democratic perspective, and were regularly shut down by the authorities, only to pop up again in another guise. Both Bakunin and Marx submitted articles to the *Deutsche Jahrbücher*, but only Bakunin's "The Reaction in Germany: A Fragment from a Frenchman" was published. That Bakunin beat Marx into print is surprising, for in his later life Bakunin was notorious for rarely finishing a writing project. Marx suffered from the same malady, but his life was more stable and with the aid of his wife Jenny and his friend Engels more of his work was completed and published. It brought Marx little money—he complained that he had spent more on cigars while writing *Capital* than he could hope to recoup in royalties. But because it was published, it was read, and that established him as an important intellectual within the labor and left movements. Bakunin's reputation after 1842 would be based less on his writing than his activism.

But until the *Communist Manifesto* of 1848 and *Capital*, published in 1867, Bakunin's article in the *Deutsche Jahrbücher* made him the better known and respected progressive thinker. It is in "The Reaction in Germany" that his most famous quote appears: "The passion for destruction is at the same time a creative passion."[4] While it is often cited by anarchists and used as a guide to action, Bakunin was not outlining tactics or gesturing towards anarchism; he was writing as a Hegelian, not an anarchist, in 1842 and not counseling a diversity of tactics or violence. It was, however, a call for "a total transformation" and the building of "an original new life which has not yet existed in history." In this Bakunin foreshadowed Marx's comment in an 1843 letter to Ruge, where he called for the "ruthless criticism of all that exists."[5] Mere tinkering with the system was not sufficient for either rebel, even if the means and ends were still unclear.

The article was important for another passage as well. Previous revolutions had only replaced one small ruling group with another. Feudal lords, for example, were replaced with capitalists and kings replaced with parliaments. The next revolution, however, would be more profound and it would be made, Bakunin argued, by "the people, the poor class," who made up "the greatest part of humanity." Revolts in France and England, and even conservative Germany, made this clear; workers and peasants had been promised much by the classes that had made previous revolutions, but had received little. If they were to obtain real freedom, economic and political freedom, with neither god nor state nor capitalist, workers would have to make the revolution themselves.

Marx was developing very similar views independently. His studies of the philosophy of law had stressed more abstract notions of justice, but the real world of politics and resistance kept intruding. As he noted years later in the preface to *A Contribution to the Critique of Political Economy*, still a valuable summary of Marx's view of the relationship of political economy to history, he was deeply influenced by the closing of the commons illustrated by prosecution of Rhenish peasants for exercising their long-held right to take wood from the forests. That example of realpolitik and others—such as self-serving parliamentary debates on free trade and tariffs, the terrible conditions of the Moselle peasants, and state censorship of the journal he helped edit, the *Rheinische Zeitung*—made it clear that the state was no impartial arbiter of conflict within society. It was instead a tool of those with economic—class—power. This observation contrasted greatly with the lofty sentiments of justice and morality espoused by politicians and philosophers. Such sentiments did not mirror reality; they hid it, providing an ideological smokescreen for class interests and exploitation. But before moving on to politics, Marx had to "settle accounts with our former philosophical conscience."[6] That meant voracious reading and writing and resulted in the *Economic and Philosophic Manuscripts*, sometimes called the *Paris Manuscripts*, where he wrote about alienation, and *The German Ideology*, written with Engels as an exposition of materialist history against the idealist histories of the Hegelians. Neither was published in his lifetime, but they are some of Marx's most interesting work.

By 1844, Bakunin and Marx were in Paris, each exiled from their homelands for their political activity. Bakunin had publically assailed the Russian government on several occasions, and was ordered to return to face trial for his remarks. He refused and was tried and convicted *in absentia*. His Russian assets, meager at best, were forfeited to the state, and he was sentenced to a term of hard labor to be served if he returned to Russia.

Marx left Germany after the authorities shut down the *Rheinische Zeitung* and headed for Paris to help Ruge set up a new journal, the *Deutsche-Franzosische Jahrbücher*. It published only one issue before the authorities shut it down, but it did contain a short note by Bakunin and longer articles by Marx. The two men finally met and traveled in the same circles, meeting and arguing with activists and writers such as Wilhelm Weitling, Louis Blanc, Pierre-Joseph Proudhon, Alexander Herzen, Ivan Turgenev, and George Sand.

Events would soon separate the two radicals. As Europe exploded into revolution in 1848, Bakunin and Marx threw themselves into the cause. Bakunin fought on the barricades in Prague, was expelled from Prussia, sneaked back to Leipzig to plan a revolt, then fought again in

Dresden, this time beside the composer Richard Wagner. Wagner fled and escaped the subsequent repression, but Bakunin was rounded up and sentenced to death. The sentence was commuted to life imprisonment, but Bakunin was soon turned over to Russia, where his previous sentence was still outstanding. He was entombed in the notorious Peter and Paul Fortress, the same prison that had held the Decembrists and would hold Dostoevsky, Nikolai Chernyshevsky, the author of the revolutionary novel *What Is to Be Done?*, the anarchist Peter Kropotkin, and Leon Trotsky. There, in 1851, Bakunin would write his so-called *Confession*, a fascinating document that combined a critique of Russia with a request for mercy without implicating any of his revolutionary comrades or betraying the cause. His appeal for leniency failed. He was transferred to Shlisselberg Fortress outside of St. Petersburg, the same prison where Lenin's brother would be hanged in 1887. There Bakunin contracted scurvy and suffered the loss of his teeth. In 1857, his sentence was commuted to exile in Siberia, where he could take up something that resembled a normal life in Tomsk, working as a French tutor. Now forty-four years old, he met and soon married Antonia Kwitakowski, a much younger woman, daughter of a Polish gold trader. The two moved to Irkutsk, and Bakunin found work with a trading company.

While Bakunin fought on the barricades, rotted in prison, and cobbled together a sparse living in exile, Marx continued to work as a journalist and political thinker. This comparison is not invidious. *The Communist Manifesto*, written with Engels in 1848, was a product of this period, as were a series of articles on political economy in his newspaper, the *Neue Rheinische Zeitung*, later published as *Wage Labor and Capital*. But he also published a baseless rumor that Bakunin was a spy for the Russian secret police, a rumor that in a period of revolutionary excess could well have had Bakunin executed by his comrades. Marx's printing of the rumor reflected his Russophobia, and in the pages of the *Neue Rheinische Zeitung*, he called for a German war against Russia to accompany the class war in

Europe. The paper was soon shut down by the authorities and Marx was hounded from Germany to France, and then, by 1850, to London.

He would spend the rest of his life there with his wife Jenny and their children, eking out a bare existence writing for newspapers and augmented with subsidies from Engels. Most of his time was devoted to the research and writing that would lead to the publication of volume one of *Capital* in 1867 and the voluminous notes and unfinished manuscripts ranging from the *Grundrisse* to two more volumes of *Capital* to the three volumes of *Theories of Surplus Value*, none of which would be published in his lifetime. He would also have a great deal of time for political intrigue.

Much of that intrigue would be aimed at Bakunin, who had escaped from his Siberian exile in 1861. He received permission to travel from Irkutsk to Nikolaevsk, ostensibly on business for his firm, then narrowly escaped arrest to board a Russian steamer. When the steamer gave a becalmed American ship a tow, Bakunin transferred to the towed vessel, and then from its port of call took another ship to Japan. He made his way to Yokohama, and from there sailed to San Francisco. At San Francisco, he took passage to the Panama isthmus, traveled overland, then sailed to New York, and thence to London, where he met fellow Russian exile and socialist Alexander Herzen.

His journey had taken six months and left him heavily in debt but eager to return to radical politics. That meant writing and throwing himself into nationalist causes from Sweden to Poland. His wife would not be able to join him for two years, but in 1864, he did meet up again with Marx in London. Their encounter went well enough— as Marx commented in a note to Engels, "I must say I liked him very much, more so than previously. . . . On the whole, he is one of the few people whom after sixteen years I find to have moved forward and not backward." In part this was because Bakunin had given up on nationalist causes such as the Polish independence movement and now considered himself first and foremost a socialist. He believed, along with Marx, that a movement to empower workers and peasants could not be based on idealist appeals to "rights." Rights had nothing to do with universal values and everything to do with power; rights did not transcend class interests, they enforced them. As Marx noted in *Capital*, "the capitalist maintains his rights as a purchaser when he tries to make the working day as long as possible . . . and the worker maintains his rights as a seller when he wishes to reduce the working day. . . . Between equal rights, force decides."[7] Bakunin agreed with this materialist conception of history and politics. His best-known publication, *God and the State*, begins:

> Who are right, the idealists or the materialists? The question once stated in this way, hesitation becomes impossible. Undoubtedly the idealists are wrong and the materialists right. Yes, facts are before ideas; yes, the ideal, as Proudhon said, is but a flower, whose root lies in the material conditions of existence. Yes, the whole history of humanity, intellectual and moral, political and social, is but a reflection of its economic history.[8]

At their brief meeting, Bakunin agreed with Marx on another point—that revolutionary activity meant fighting for socialism and that he would carry on the fight within the new organization to which Marx belonged: the International Working Men's Association.

The story of their acrimonious feud within the International has been told and retold in great detail for more than 150 years, with anarchists and Marxists putting each utterance, every platform, every gesture and aside under a microscope, searching for evidence to exculpate and convict. It is not, however, an argument that can be finally resolved—there is no proof that will convince all sides. Ultimately, the fight in the International and after is a sad story with no victors, a story of two great thinkers and activists mired in schism and antipathy, a story of misapprehension and missed opportunities. It is not an unfamiliar story on the left. The writer and film director John Sayles has poked fun at it with compassion and wit. In his short story "At the

Anarchists' Convention" a factional fight breaks out and the story's narrator observes, "Whatever drove man to split the atom is the engine that rules their lives. Not divide and conquer but divide and subdivide."[9]

Why such bitter fighting between two radicals who had so much in common, from their backgrounds and educations to their philosophical views to politics? The issues over which they publically differed provide no real answers. With the benefit of hindsight, they seem rather trivial, the sorts of things reasonable minds might agree to differ over and put aside for the larger cause. Split the International on the question of inheritance under socialism? On the correct response to religion and atheism among the working class? I would go even further, to ask whether they were as fundamentally opposed on the larger issues of organization, authority, reform, and the state as generations of anarchists and Marxists have insisted. Both Bakunin and Marx, and their followers, have too often pulled a phrase from the other's writing and built a ferocious critique on a fragment. Assessing what either "really meant" or believed on an issue requires a much deeper reading and discussion than either Bakunin or Marx was interested in doing, or than many of those who follow them are interested in doing. Marx was wrong to insist Bakunin believed that revolutions were made only by will, that material conditions meant nothing. We look in vain for evidence that Marx argues for a repressive state or even a vanguard party. Many of their differences were based on the most uncharitable reading of the other's work and the maligning of the other's motives, and some of these errors continue to inform debate today.

It may, therefore, be instructive to consider other reasons for the intensity of their fight in the International. It is worth noting that they never met again after their 1864 meeting in London; their moves and countermoves were fought via proxy, circular, editorial, and plot, never through open debate and discussion. Like an internet spat today, that practically guaranteed misreading, misunderstanding, misapprehension, adrenaline dumps, and bitter polemics that raise the temperature but provides little illumination.

At another level, it may be that their very similarities made reconciliation and solidarity difficult. The writer Russell Jacoby in *Bloodlust: On the Roots of Violence from Cain and Abel to the Present* argues that violence is, contrary to popular impression, more likely to occur between people who know each other. Building on Sigmund Freud's insight of the narcissism of minor differences, Jacoby writes, "We know their faults, their beliefs, their desires, and we distrust them *because* of that."[10]

Jacoby is concerned with violence, not political schisms, but there may be a lesson applicable to the International there. Both Bakunin and Marx reacted like greyhounds to a starting pistol at the chance for political intrigue and scheming. Each desired to be respected and appreciated by the revolutionary movement. In their delight in parsing the other's ideas and actions to highlight and heighten what seemed irreconcilable differences of principle, motive, and strategy, it is hard not to see this as efforts to "brand" their politics and win supporters. It is, after all, when manufacturers are competing to sell very similar products that they intensify their advertising. Political figures, who need to move others to action, likewise are prone to stress difference rather than commonality when staking out a position. In his book *Rules for Radicals: A Pragmatic Primer for Realistic Radicals* the organizer Saul Alinsky notes that the American Declaration of Independence did not list any of the benefits the colonists received from the British Empire. Such a list might have revealed that there was only a 20 percent difference between the Empire and the colony, and no one was going to pick up a gun for such a slight difference. To move people, Alinsky continues, "Our cause had to be all shining justice, allied with the angels; theirs had to be all evil, tied to the Devil; in no war has the enemy or the cause ever been gray."[11] That Bakunin and Marx would adopt such tactics against each other instead of capital and the state may be sad and deplorable, but it is hardly new or startling.

It is, however, easy to overstate their similarities. Their lives differed greatly after the revolutionary period of the 1840s and they learned different lessons from their different experiences. His Russian imprisonment and exile gave Bakunin little faith in the possibility of reforming the state. In London, Marx had the opportunity to appreciate the gains British workers had made through reform, notably the passage of the Ten Hours Act that limited the length of the workday. The relative liberality of the British state contrasted sharply with that of autocratic Russia and each radical drew different lessons from their experience about how the revolution would be made and who would make it.

At the same time, the failure of the revolutionary moment of 1848 and the reaction that followed imbued many with pessimism, much as the failure of 1968 pushed another generation of activists to conservatism and scholasticism and a deep distrust of the working class. Alexander Herzen never recovered from the defeats of '48 and became cautious and suspicious, especially when confronted with new generations of radicals. Marx turned from activism to analysis and spent many of the next years in the British Library. Bakunin, however, emerged from prison with his revolutionary zeal untempered by the reaction of 1848 and the bitter decade that followed it. For good and ill, he had not learned the same lessons as those who had remained in the world. Thus he was easily taken in by the unscrupulous Russian murderer and revolutionary Sergei Nechaev, author of the amoral "Catechism of a Revolutionary." More cynical radicals and reformers remained deeply and rightly suspicious of the young militant, while Bakunin initially thought he saw in him the spark of rebellion that had been snuffed out among the politicos of his own generation. Marx, meanwhile, had learned patience, however distasteful waiting may have been. One lesson that might be taken from the failure of '48 was the revolution would not be made with enthusiasm alone, and the possibilities of reform in the meantime seemed worth working for. The rebel energy Bakunin exuded filled Marx with alarm and suspicion, for it seemed naive and foolhardy, exposing the movement to repression for no appreciable gain. Bakunin in turn saw

Marx's analysis and patience as a way to derail the revolution and empower the bureaucrat and the party, for it seemed to imply that those who understood history and laws of dialectical change, not the people, should determine the timing and methods of revolution.

Bakunin was undoubtedly correct and perceptive to see in Marx's work the potential for authoritarians and intellectuals to use the revolutionary movement and historical materialism to catapult themselves into power with catastrophic results. In *God and the State* and in his last work, *Statism and Anarchy*, we find brilliant passages that offer prescient warnings of the horrors of state socialism—or, depending on one's perspective, state capitalism. As the novelist Walter Mosley put it in the novella "Walking the Line," Bakunin "knew about all the gross injustices of Stalin before Stalin was born. He was probably the greatest political thinker of the twentieth century and he didn't even live in that century."[12] That Bakunin's vision could make its way even into modern detective fiction demonstrates his ability to quickly sum up a situation, to see the underlying direction of ideas and events and extrapolate from them. As Herzen noted, "as soon as he had grasped two or three features of his surroundings, he singled out the revolutionary current and at once set to work to carry it farther, to expand it, making of it the burning question of life."[13]

But it must be noted that Bakunin's criticism of what would become the Marxism of Stalin and Lenin was not based on a careful analysis of what Marx wrote or did. Bakunin's predictions were based on a very partial reading of Marx. For every quote one might produce to suggest Marx was a strict historical determinist, such as the famous quote from *The Poverty of Philosophy*, that "the hand-mill gives you society with the feudal lord; the steam-mill society with the industrial capitalist," we may find quotes "proving" the opposite. For example, in *The Holy Family*, published in 1845, we find Marx and Engels writing "*History* does *nothing*, it 'possesses *no* immense wealth,' it 'wages *no* battles.' It is *man*, real, living man who does all that, who possesses and fights; 'history' is not, as it were, a person apart, using man as a means to achieve *its own* aims; history is *nothing but* the activity of man pursuing his aims."[14] Which is the "real" Marx? It depends on the ends of the reader. That writers and activists from Rosa Luxemburg to E.P. Thompson to Paul Mattick to Ralph Miliband to Maurice Brinton to Ellen Meiksins Wood could work within a Marxist tradition and come to very different, antiauthoritarian conclusions about the state than Leninists, Stalinists, Trotskyists, and social democrats is surely proof that Bakunin's reading is not the only possible one.[15]

Nor is there is any evidence for the anarchist claim that Marx was an authoritarian statist who sought to replace the ruling class with a cadre of intellectuals to create the horrors of Leninism and Stalinism. There is no doubt, however, that Marx was a ferocious, even unscrupulous debater, often a bully who did not suffer fools gladly. He jumped on his opponents with the zeal of the professional pedant and deployed every rhetorical trick to refute, expose, and ridicule them. It was never an endearing trait and could easily degenerate to unscrupulously attributing false motives and making false accusations. There was, for example, nothing to the claims of Marx and some Marxists that Bakunin was a plotter who wanted to undermine the International and replace its leaders, including Marx, with a conspiratorial cabal led by himself. The accusations by Marxists that Bakunin was a spy were a particularly odious charge. But it is very far from the name-calling and machinations of the International to the Cheka and the gulag, and nothing in Marx's writing or actions supports any claim that he is any more responsible for them than Christ is responsible for the Spanish Inquisition or Jim Jones. And it is hardly the case that Bakunin was immune to the siren call of invective and slander.

It is the case that the two had very different personalities. Despite the similarities in their education and evolution through philosophy, despite their overlapping ideas and friends, despite the comradely atmosphere of revolutionary Europe, the two did not get along. Bakunin had enjoyed their "instructive and lively" conversations, but while they "were friendly enough . . . we were never really close. Our temperaments did not allow it. He called me a sentimental idealist, and he was right. I called him vain, treacherous, and cunning, and I too was right."[16]

While Bakunin's characterizations need not be taken at face value, differences in temperament may be more important than they seem. As the American anarchist Voltairine de Cleyre once observed, politics is often an expression of one's temperament. Put another way, how we react to events and challenges, how we think about tactics and strategies, is as often shaped by our personalities, our emotional responses, our personal strengths and weaknesses, as by the application of reason and logic. Thus there may be something to be learned from considering the ways the personalities and temperaments of Bakunin and Marx shaped their work in the movement.[17]

Bakunin's intellectual strength was that of a broad synthesizer who would overlook details and small errors in search of a greater truth, better able to pen the evocative phrase and the more powerful image than unearth the empirical data and construct a tight argument. Inspiring people was more important than strict logic, popularizing more important than precision. He was not much interested in scoring academic points against comrades. In contrast, Marx was a careful scholar who took his research very seriously, chasing down evidence, refining arguments, anticipating and defeating criticism, and writing with exactitude. Bakunin summed up the differences when he reflected upon their early years, writing, "I knew nothing then about political economy, I had not given up metaphysical abstractions, and my socialism was only instinctive." In contrast, Marx was "a well-informed materialist and a reflective socialist . . . much more advanced than I was."[18] Bakunin's remarks say something important about the two men and the way they worked in the movement.

We can see this in their relationships with other radicals of the 1840s, notably Wilhelm Weitling and Pierre-Joseph Proudhon. Though only a few years older than Bakunin and Marx, they represented a previous generation of radicals. Weitling was a tailor by trade, Proudhon a printer. Both were largely self-educated; neither was an intellectual trained as Bakunin and Marx had been trained. They wrote not for the academy, but for workers and artisans and peasants, and were respected figures on the left as much for their actions as for their intellectual thought. Both preferred the dramatic statement to the carefully reasoned, footnoted argument. Proudhon's answer to the question of the title of his 1840 book, *What Is Property?*, still resonates today: Property is theft!

Bakunin and Marx were deeply influenced by Weitling and Proudhon, even as they were aware of their shortcomings as thinkers. It is in their actions toward them that we see some indication of their very different temperaments. For his part, Bakunin observed that Weitling did not understand political economy and that Proudhon never left abstract ideas of right and justice for materialism, never came to see that "that economic fact has always preceded legal and political right." But however imprecise their logic and arguments might be, Bakunin continued to appreciate Weitling and Proudhon for their passion and dedication to the cause and felt no need to attack them for insufficient intellectual rigor.

It is often remarked that in academia the fights are so fierce because the stakes are so small. In the best and worst traditions of the academy, Marx could not let error go unrefuted and was quick to appoint himself arbiter. Competing with Weitling for the ideological leadership of a small group of radicals, Marx denounced him at a meeting, shouting, "Ignorance has never yet helped anyone!" and attacked Weitling in left and labor circles. He then turned on Proudhon, who had recently published a new book, *The System of Economic Contradictions; or, The Philosophy of Poverty*. In it, Proudhon attempted to combine the Hegelian insights he had gleaned from Bakunin and Marx with his own views on political economy. Marx wrote a 160-page critique called *The Poverty of Philosophy*, the inverted title itself a jab at Proudhon's ill-digested Hegelianism. Marx's opening remarks set the sarcastic tone for his critique:

M. Proudhon has the misfortune of being peculiarly misunderstood in Europe. In France, he has the right to be a bad economist, because he is reputed to be a good German philosopher. In Germany, he has the right to be a bad philosopher, because he is reputed to be one of the ablest French economists. Being both German and an economist at the same time, we desire to protest against this double error.[19]

The Poverty of Philosophy was clever and pointed, and in his lengthy critique of Proudhon Marx worked out some of the principles of his materialist philosophy that Bakunin admired and shared. But it was tawdry treatment of someone who had done much for the movement and much to shape Marx's own thinking. For his part, Bakunin largely agreed with the substance of Marx's critique, but preferred to keep silent rather than score scholastic points against a comrade. Relationships and revolutionary spirit were more important to him than ferociously refuting error.

There is more to this difference than a reminder that the personal can become the political in negative ways. People play different roles in social movements, and these roles inform their responses to tactical and strategic questions. The roles themselves often reflect temperaments and experiences. The contemporary activists Bill Moyer and George Lakey developed a training tool that demonstrates this. It has people take up one of four roles needed in every movement—helpers, organizers, rebels, educators—and explore the differences and antagonisms between them.[20] Because these roles are often rooted in our experiences, it is remarkably easy to see one's own role as crucial and correct and to discount the others. Rebels can easily disparage the educators, for everyone knows that theory minus action equals zero. Organizers may become angry with rebels who may demonstrate revolutionary daring but drive away potential allies. Helpers may see educational work as diverting attention from people who need assistance now, not in some utopian future. Educators may despair that their careful work is ignored, leading to crippling contradictions in thought and deed. And so on. Such divisions can generate spontaneously, quickly, and ferociously because they often stem from our personalities, from who we are in the world. A contrary view can feel like an attack on our selves, and we respond accordingly.

If Bakunin's primary role was that of rebel, that of Marx was educator. Such differences might have been combined to reinforce each other; that is how successful movements develop. But overcoming the differences takes a great deal of work. It was not work either Bakunin or Marx was inclined to do.

It may be work worth doing now. It does not require ignoring the lessons of Kronstadt, of the purges, forced collectivization, and other state violence perpetrated by vicious self-perpetuating elites acting in the name of Marx. Bakunin, after all, was undeniably accurate in his predictions about the corrupting effect of political power and in reminding us that "when the people are being beaten with a stick, they are not much happier if it is called 'the People's stick.'"[21] At the same time it does not mean ignoring the lessons from the political and ethical failures of the anarchist "illegalists" and the *attentats* and bombings of the late nineteenth and early twentieth centuries.

Nor does it mean there are no significant differences between anarchism and Marxism. Indeed, as many have pointed out, debates between anarchists and Marxists have often been fruitful and inspiring to both sides. For example, Marx's later letters to Russian revolutionaries and his *Critique of the Gotha Program* demonstrate his evolving views on the possibilities of revolution and reform, some of which seemed to reflect Bakunin's influence, especially the realization that a rapidly industrializing Russia, not western Europe, might be the first country to launch a social revolution, and that the peasantry as well as the working class could be a revolutionary agent. For Bakunin, the internecine war in the International let him use his considerable talent for deduction and synthesis to develop his critique of intellectuals, the vanguard, and the state. Subsequent commentators have demonstrated how interactions and debates between anarchists and Marxists have shaped both movements.[22] But social movements require mass participation, and that requires collaboration on positions and understanding temperaments, including our own. It does not mean compromising or giving up crucial and defining principles. It does mean taking some care in defining what those principles are and examining them in the light of our personalities, our egos, and our social roles, as well as the specific historical moments we are in and the specific tactical and strategic possibilities we have.

The lives of Bakunin and Marx did not conclude with their feud in the International, though their active political lives peaked then. For a dispute that took up so much of their lives, it produced very little save division and distrust. When the fighting finally ended in 1872 with Marx's success in purging Bakunin from the International and the subsequent creation of an anarchist international, the two were in their fifties and were plagued by personal tragedy and ill health, much of it the consequence of the poverty that marked both their lives. Both largely withdrew from active politics and turned to writing. Their articles on the Paris Commune of 1871 still have much to offer historians and activists, though they are too often heaped up as ammunition for one side or the other. Bakunin's *Statism and Anarchy* was published in 1873, and he announced his retirement from the revolutionary struggle later that year. Bakunin died in Switzerland on July 1, 1876, aged sixty-two; Marx, devastated by the death of his wife Jenny in 1881 and his daughter two years later, would himself die in 1883, aged sixty-four. Each of their funerals was sparsely attended, and their graves would go unmarked until supporters could raise funds for markers. Neither had any idea of how their lives, their writing, even their feud, would continue to shape the world. Yet contemporary activists can learn a great deal about our world from their work, and perhaps something about building a new world from their fight. The useful discussions between anarchists and Marxists about the International will not be over who was right but over how we might do better within our organizations and communities today.

BIBLIOGRAPHY AND FURTHER READING

BAKUNIN'S LIFE AND IDEAS ARE EXAMINED IN MY *BAKUNIN: THE CREATIVE Passion*, published by St. Martin's Press, 2006, and in paperback by Seven Stories Press, 2009. An excellent analysis of Bakunin's journey through philosophy may be found in Paul McLaughlin, *Mikhail Bakunin: The Philosophical Basis of His Anarchism* (Algora, 2002). Life at Priamukhino is investigated in depth by John Randolph in *The House in the Garden: The Bakunin Family and the Romance of Russian Idealism* (Cornell University Press, 2007). E.H. Carr's *Michael Bakunin* (1937; Vintage Books, 1971) is a detailed look at Bakunin's life but does not discuss his ideas or politics. Those matters are explored sympathetically in Brian Morris's *Bakunin: The Philosophy of Freedom* (Black Rose Books, 1993) and Richard B. Saltman's *The Social and Political Thought of Michael Bakunin* (Greenwood Press, 1983).

Bakunin's own work is, to date, available in English only in various edited collections. His complete works are available on *Bakounine: Oeuvres complètes* (Amsterdam: International Institute of Social History, 2000, CD-ROM). Bakunin's most extensive published piece, the book-length *Statism and Anarchy*, was first published in Russian rather than Bakunin's usual French. The best English edition is translated and edited by Marshall Shatz (Cambridge University Press, 1990), though in my assessment, he cedes too much to Bakunin's critics who accuse him of anti-Semitism.

The best English biography of Marx by an academic historian is David McLellan, *Karl Marx*, originally published in 1973 and now in its fourth edition. Jonathan Sperber's *Karl Marx: A Nineteenth Century Life* (W.W. Norton, 2013) has nothing new to say about Marx and is colored by the author's view that Marx's economic ideas have no relevance today. It does offer a useful, broad context of revolutionary nineteenth-century Europe. Two lively biographies by journalists are Francis Wheen, *Karl Marx: A Life* (Fourth Estate, 1999) and Mary Gabriel, *Love and Capital: Karl and Jenny Marx and the Birth of a Revolution* (New York: Little, Brown, 2011). Wheen is brisk and amusing, but he presents a caricature of Bakunin that shows no sign of the author having read anything by or about Bakunin apart from the silliest Marxist critiques. Neither book makes a serious effort to engage with Marx's ideas. The biography by Franz Mehring, a member of the Spartacus League, *Karl Marx: The Story of His Life*, first published in 1918 and translated into English in 1935, is an insightful biography that is sympathetic to Bakunin.

1 Michael Bakunin, "Preface to Hegel's *Gymnasium Lectures*," 1838, and "On Philosophy," in *Bakounine: Oeuvres complètes* (Amsterdam: International Institute of Social History, 2000), CD-ROM.

2 Karl Marx and Friedrich Engels, "The German Ideology," in *Collected Works*, vol. 5 (New York: International Publishers, 1976), 236.

3 Bakunin, "Preface to Hegel's *Gymnasium Lectures*."

4 The article is available in many places, including online, with the phrase translated in slightly different ways. The original German in *Bakounine: Oeuvres complètes* is "Die Lust der Zerstörung ist zugliech eine schaffende Lust."

5 "Marx to Arnold Ruge, September 1843," in *Collected Works*, vol. 3 (1975), 142.

6 Marx, Preface to "A Contribution to the Critique of Political Economy," in *Collected Works*, vol. 29 (1987), 264.

7 Marx, *Capital: A Critique of Political Economy*, trans. Ben Fowkes (London: Penguin Books, 1990), 344.

8 Bakunin, *God and the State* (New York: Dover, 1970), 9.

9 John Sayles, "At the Anarchists' Convention," in *The Anarchists' Convention and Other Stories* (New York: Nation Books, 1979), 24.

10 Russell Jacoby, *Bloodlust: On the Roots of Violence from Cain and Abel to the Present* (New York: Free Press, 2011), x.

11 Saul D. Alinsky, *Rules for Radicals: A Pragmatic Primer for Realistic Radicals* (New York: Vintage Books, 1972), 28.

12 Walter Mosley, "Walking the Line," in *Transgressions*, ed. Ed McBain (New York: Forge, 2005), 149.

13 Alexander Herzen, *My Past and Thoughts*, trans. Constance Garnett, rev. Humphrey Higgens, vol. 3 (New York: Knopf, 1968), 1357, 1366.

14 Marx, "The Poverty of Philosophy: Answer to the *Philosophy of Poverty* by M. Proudhon," in *Collected Works*, vol. 6 (1976), 166; Marx and Engels, "The Holy Family, or Critique of Critical Criticism," in *Collected Works*, vol. 4 (1975), 93.

15 See, for example, Rosa Luxemburg, *The Russian Revolution and Leninism or Marxism?* (Ann Arbor: University of Michigan Press, 1961); E.P. Thompson, *The Making of the English Working Class* (London: Penguin, 1963); Paul Mattick, *Anti-Bolshevik Communism* (London: Merlin Press, 1978); Ralph Miliband, *The State in Capitalist Society* (London: Merlin Press, 2009); Maurice Brinton, *For Workers' Power: The Selected Works of Maurice Brinton*, ed. David Goodway (Oakland, CA: AK Press, 2004); Ellen Meiksins Wood, *Democracy against Capitalism: Renewing Historical Materialism* (London: Verso, 2016). The list might easily be expanded to include, for example, Daniel Guérin, Anton Pannekoek, and many others.

16 Bakunin, "Rapports personnels avec Marx: Pièces justificatives," in *Bakounine: Oeuvres complètes*, 1871.

17 De Cleyre's observation is more fine-grained than work by contemporary writers such as the cognitive linguist George Lakoff. Lakoff's analysis of American voters as either conservatives shaped by "strict father" families or progressives shaped by "nurturant parents" is not applicable to the differences between Bakunin and Marx. See, for example, George P. Lakoff, *Moral Politics: How Liberals and Conservatives Think* (Chicago: University of Chicago Press, 2002).

18 Bakunin, "Rapports personnels avec Marx: Pieces justicatives."

19 Marx, "The Poverty of Philosophy," 109.

20 A version of this exercise may be found on the website of Training for Change, https://www.trainingforchange.org/tools/tornado-warning-four-roles-social-change, accessed June 14, 2015. In different iterations, the roles are defined slightly differently. See, for example, George Lakey, "What Role Were

You Born to Play in Social Change?" his February 3, 2016, "Living Revolution" column at the Waging Nonviolence website, http://wagingnonviolence.org/feature/bill-moyer-four-roles-of-social-change/ accessed February 5, 2016. See also George Lakey, *Facilitating Group Learning: Strategies for Success with Diverse Adult Learners* (San Francisco: Jossey-Bass, 2010).

21 This popularized quotation is from *Statism and Anarchy*. It is rendered somewhat differently in Shatz's translation: "It will scarcely be any easier on the people if the cudgel with which they are beaten is called the people's cudgel," 23.

22 See, for example, Anthony D'Agostino, *Marxism and the Russian Anarchists* (San Francisco: Germinal Press, 1977); Alvin Gouldner, *Against Fragmentation: The Origins of Marxism and the Sociology of Intellectuals* (London: Oxford University Press, 1985); Robert Graham, *"We Do Not Fear Anarchy—We Invoke It": The First International and the Origins of the Anarchist Movement* (Oakland, CA: AK Press, 2015). The most engaging and fruitful discussion of the dynamic between Marxists and anarchists, fraught with ideas for contemporary struggles, is Kristin Ross, *Communal Luxury: The Political Imaginary of the Paris Commune* (London: Verso, 2015), see 77–89 for the evolution of Marx's thought in light of the Commune.

PM Press was founded at the end of 2007 by a small collection of folks with decades of publishing, media, and organizing experience. PM Press co-conspirators have published and distributed hundreds of books, pamphlets, CDs, and DVDs. Members of PM have founded enduring book fairs, spearheaded victorious tenant organizing campaigns, and worked closely with bookstores, academic conferences, and even rock bands to deliver political and challenging ideas to all walks of life. We're old enough to know what we're doing and young enough to know what's at stake.

We seek to create radical and stimulating fiction and non-fiction books, pamphlets, T-shirts, visual and audio materials to entertain, educate, and inspire you. We aim to distribute these through every available channel with every available technology, whether that means you are seeing anarchist classics at our bookfair stalls; reading our latest vegan cookbook at the café; downloading geeky fiction e-books; or digging new music and timely videos from our website.

PM Press is always on the lookout for talented and skilled volunteers, artists, activists, and writers to work with. If you have a great idea for a project or can contribute in some way, please get in touch.

PM Press
PO Box 23912
Oakland CA 94623
510-658-3906
www.pmpress.org

Friends of PM

These are indisputably momentous times—the financial system is melting down globally and the Empire is stumbling. Now more than ever there is a vital need for radical ideas.

In the many years since its founding—and on a mere shoestring—PM Press has risen to the formidable challenge of publishing and distributing knowledge and entertainment for the struggles ahead. With hundreds of releases to date, we have published an impressive and stimulating array of literature, art, music, politics, and culture. Using every available medium, we've succeeded in connecting those hungry for ideas and information to those putting them into practice.

Friends of PM allows you to directly help impact, amplify, and revitalize the discourse and actions of radical writers, filmmakers, and artists. It provides us with a stable foundation from which we can build upon our early successes and provides a much-needed subsidy for the materials that can't necessarily pay their own way. You can help make that happen—and receive every new title automatically delivered to your door once a month—by joining as a Friend of PM Press. And, we'll throw in a free T-Shirt when you sign up.

Here are your options:
- $30 a month: Get all books and pamphlets plus 50% discount on all webstore purchases
- $40 a month: Get all PM Press releases plus 50% discount on all webstore purchases
- $100 a month: Superstar—Everything plus PM merchandise, free downloads, and 50% discount on all webstore purchases

For those who can't afford $30 or more a month, we have **Sustainer Rates** at $15, $10 and $5. Sustainers get a free PM Press T-shirt and a 50% discount on all purchases from our website.

Your Visa or Mastercard will be billed once a month, until you tell us to stop. Or until our efforts succeed in bringing the revolution around. Or the financial meltdown of Capital makes plastic redundant. Whichever comes first.

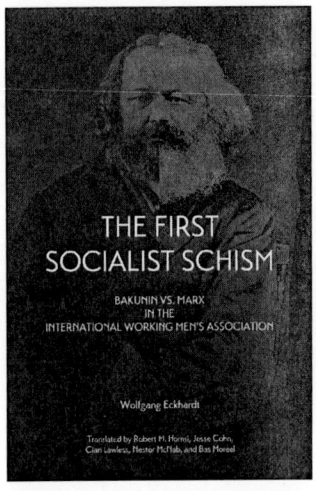

THE FIRST
SOCIALIST SCHISM

BAKUNIN VS. MARX
IN THE
INTERNATIONAL WORKING MEN'S ASSOCIATION

Wolfgang Eckhardt

Translated by Robert M. Homsi, Jesse Cohn,
Cian Lawless, Hester McFlab, and Bas Moreel

The First Socialist Schism
Bakunin vs. Marx in the International Working Men's Association
Wolfgang Eckhardt

$38.95 • ISBN: 978-1-62963-042-7
9x6 • 624 pages

The First Socialist Schism chronicles the conflicts in the International Working Men's Association (the First International, 1864–1877), which represents an important milestone in the history of political ideas and socialist theory. In defending their autonomy, federations in the International became aware of what separated them from the social democratic movement that relied on the establishment of national labor parties and the conquest of political power. This can be seen as a decisive moment in the history of political ideas: the split between centralist party politics and the federalist grassroots movement. The separate movements in the International—which would later develop into social democracy, communism, and anarchism—found their greatest advocates in Mikhail Bakunin and Karl Marx. However, the significance of this alleged clash of titans is largely a modern invention. It was not the rivalry between two arch-enemies or a personal vendetta based on mutual resentment that made the conflict between Bakunin and Marx so important but rather that it heralded the first socialist schism between parliamentary party politics aiming to conquer political power and social-revolutionary concepts.

Instead of focusing exclusively on what Marx and Bakunin said, many other contributions to this debate are examined, making this the first reconstruction of a dispute that gripped the entire organization. This book also provides the first detailed account of the International's Congress of The Hague (September, 1872); including the background, the sequence of events, and international reaction. The book sets new standards when it comes to source material, taking into account documents from numerous archives and libraries that have previously gone unnoticed or were completely unknown.

> "Eckhardt provides an in-depth description of the development and political context of the conflict between Marx and Bakunin. The book sets a new standard, providing a detailed account of the context, background, and effect of the conflict."
> —Jochen Schmück, DadA (Database of German-Language Anarchism)